D0574624

ANCIENT CIVILIZATIONS

THE
EGYPTIANS
BUILDERS OF THE PYRAMIDS

by
KATHERINE REECE

Publishing LLC
Vero Beach, Florida 32964

www.rourkepublishing.com

PHOTO CREDITS:
Courtesy Charles Reasoner: pages 13, 24, 27; Courtesy Corel Stock Photos: Cover, title, pages 21, 30, 43; Courtesy www.egyptiangiftshop.com: pages 36, 37, 38, 39; Courtesy www.eoluk.co.uk: page 11; Courtesy www.fiu.edu: pages 19, 38; Courtesy www.freestockphotos.com: pages 4, 10, 11, 12, 14, 17, 19, 20, 26, 27, 32, 34, 42; Courtesy www.kingtutshop.com: page 29; Courtesy Library of Congress, Prints and Photographs Division: pages 16, 33; Courtesy NASA: page 7; Courtesy R. Pelisson, www.saharamet.com: page 8; Courtesy Ehab Samy, www.ehabweb.net: page 8; Courtesy www.touregypt.com: pages 15, 41.

DESIGN AND LAYOUT: ROHM PADILLA
RESEARCH/PAGINATION: SANDY HUGHES

Library of Congress Cataloging-in-Publication Data

Reece, Katherine E., 1955-
    The Egyptians: builders of the pyramids / Katherine Reece.
            p. c.m. -- (Ancient Civilizations)
    Includes bibliographical references and index.
    ISBN 1-59515-505-8 (hardcover)

TITLE PAGE IMAGE
A close-up of the face on the Great Sphinx at Giza

Printed in the USA.

Table of Contents

INTRODUCTION

Bathing may be routine for you, but do you know when bathrooms were first added to homes? Women wear makeup today, but do you know when color was first put on someone's face and why? You see tunnels through mountain highways, but what purpose did early tunnels serve?

Egyptian kings and pharaohs were buried in stone coffins and placed in tombs.

Who first thought of preserving dead bodies and why?

Answers to these questions can be found by studying one of the earliest and greatest civilizations, which had its beginnings along the Nile River in Egypt. The people of this civilization, which lasted for almost 3,000 years, created a national government, developed basic forms of writing using pictures, and invented paper. Egyptians had one of the first religions to emphasize life after death and developed the science of preserving bodies. Reminders of the glory of ancient Egypt still stand today in the form of pyramids that were built as tombs for their rulers.

CHAPTER 1:
WHERE IS EGYPT?

Egypt is a long, narrow, fertile country located in the northeast corner of Africa. To the north, the country widens into the area known as the Delta, or Lower Egypt, and covers almost 4,250 square miles (11,000 sq km). In the south is Upper Egypt, known as the Valley, which stretches for 660 miles (1,060 km) in length. Egypt covers 386,662 square miles (1,001,268 sq km) and is slightly more than three times the size of New Mexico in the United States.

The longest river in the world divides Egypt in half. The Nile River is more than 4,000 miles (6,437 km) long; 600 (966 km) of those miles run through Egypt. The Nile flows north out of the heart of central Africa through the dunes and cliffs of the Egyptian desert to form a narrow ribbon of water between green fields, before it empties into the Mediterranean Sea.

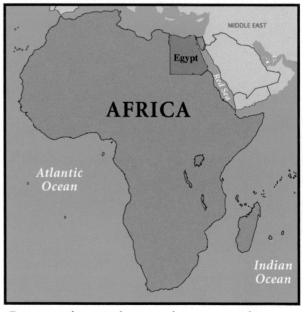

Egypt is located in northeastern Africa.

THE LONGEST RIVER IN THE WORLD

The Nile River resembles a **lotus** flower, which was an ancient symbol for regeneration of life. The long, narrow Nile River valley represented the stem, and the delta that spreads out in the shape of a triangle is the flower. In the middle of Egypt is the "bud" of the flower in a region known today as Al Fayyum.

The Nile River

Egypt's climate is very hot and dry with almost no rainfall. On the coast, occasional rains leave up to 8 inches (20 cm) annually, but inland a mere inch (2.5 cm) is more normal. Winter temperatures in the Delta range from 65°F (18°C) to 74°F (23°C), and summer temperatures are from 96°F (36°C) to 106°F (41°C). The desert temperatures vary from highs of 104°F (40°C) during the day to lows of 45°F (7°C) at night.

Camels can travel long distances across the desert without water.

Ancient Egypt drew its life from the Nile River, and people who settled in the area depended on its annual floods. Each summer the Nile overflowed onto the land during the **inundation**. From mid-July through October, water covered the river banks, and a layer of rich, dark soil was left behind. The desert turned into a land where crops could grow, animals could graze, and civilization could develop.

A modern view of the Nile River delta shows rich green farmland surrounded by desert.

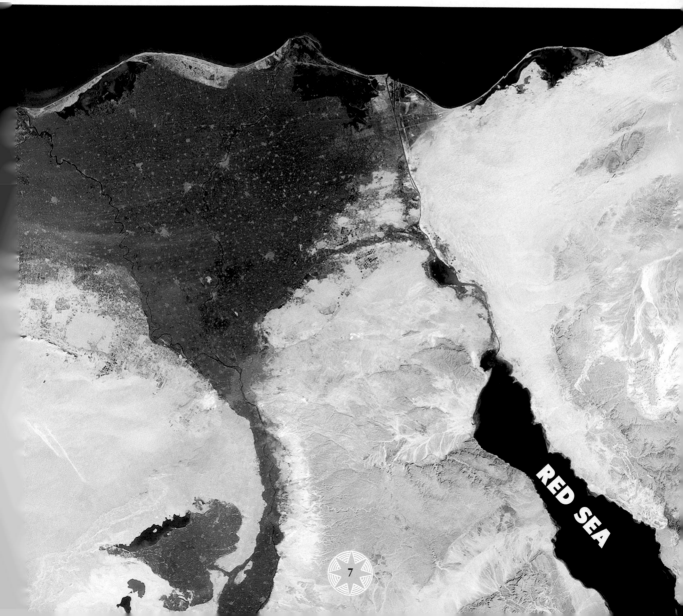

RED SEA

The towering red mountains of the Sinai Desert are surrounded by deep valleys.

On Egypt's east, south, and west borders were deserts that provided protection from invaders. The Sahara Desert on Egypt's western border is divided into two sections by the Nile River. The Western Desert covers two thirds of Egypt, and the Eastern Desert is rich with minerals and gems.

Egypt's diverse landscape has mountains, deserts, and low-lying lands near the Mediterranean Sea. In the southern Sinai Desert, mountain peaks reach to heights of 8,651 feet (2,637 m). The lowest point of land is 436 feet (133 m) *below* sea level!

The largest desert in the world, the Sahara spreads across most of North Africa covering an area roughly the size of the United States.

CHAPTER II

WHO WERE THE EGYPTIANS?

More than 5,000 years ago the Sahara Desert was a well-watered plain. Over time the climate changed, and the land dried. People who roamed the desert for their food were forced to search for water. As early as 5000 B.C.E., people began to settle in villages on the banks of the Nile River.

These early farmers worked together to set up a system to bring water from the Nile River to their fields in order to grow crops. Flooding provided plenty of water between July and October, but by digging canals and ditches farmers were able to save enough water to last the whole year. With the water they stored, farmers were able to grow two crops each year instead of one. They grew grains such as wheat and barley and began to tame the wild sheep and goats in the area.

Wheat is a grain from which flour for baking bread is made.

By 4000 B.C.E., as villages grew, the development of crafts and tools using bronze, copper, and slate found in the surrounding desert lands increased. Mud brick walls surrounded small towns in 3500 B.C.E., and tombs were built for local rulers. The Kingdom of Egypt had developed into two distinct areas called Lower Egypt along the Nile Delta and Upper Egypt in the southern section. By 3300 B.C.E., each land had its own god, and the rulers were identified by the crowns they wore–the Red Crown in Lower Egypt and the White Crown in Upper Egypt.

A form of writing that used pictures for sounds and ideas was invented around 3300 B.C.E. These **hieroglyphs**, meaning "speech of the gods," were used to make lasting records. Hieroglyphs were written on wet clay tablets that were then baked in the sun.

The mud brick walls of Karnak

Egyptians used pictures to write in a language known as hieroglyphs.

With the invention of **papyrus**, the first paper, Egyptians were able to do away with clumsy clay tablets. Writing could now be done with a brush and ink on paper scrolls that were rolled and stored or sent with messengers over great distances. With the growth of cities and government, the need for record keeping increased as Egyptian rulers gathered their many possessions.

MAKING THE FIRST PAPER

Papyrus was made from a reedlike plant that grew in the marshes along the Nile River. First the outer layer was peeled away, and the core was sliced. After the strips were soaked in water, they were drained, arranged in criss-crossed layers, and then covered with linen. The sheets were hammered flat with a stone and mallet and dried. The sap from the papyrus stuck the strips together to form paper.

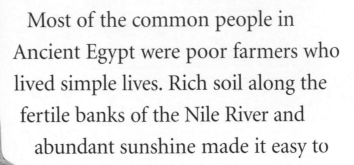

Statue of a
woman grinding corn

Most of the common people in Ancient Egypt were poor farmers who lived simple lives. Rich soil along the fertile banks of the Nile River and abundant sunshine made it easy to grow crops. All land was owned by the **pharaoh**, but the common people farmed the land and gave a portion of their crops to their rulers. Most of the time they could depend on annual flooding to provide for good harvests. However, if the waters were too high or low, villages would be under water or the fields would not get enough nutrients, resulting in **famine**.

A farmer's house was small with an entrance hall, living room, kitchen, and bedrooms with little furniture. During the day the thick mud walls absorbed heat from the hot desert and at night released their warmth as protection against the cool nights. Working the land was the farmer's life, except during the inundation when they were called to work on the public monuments. They were paid in food, oil, cloth, and other necessities, thus providing a good income between the sowing and harvesting of crops. Most children worked alongside their parents with no time for school.

A typical farmer's house

In contrast, wealthier Egyptians lived in very comfortable homes with shaded courtyards and shallow pools filled with colorful fish. Musicians played and danced around the pool for the family's enjoyment. In a hot, dry, dusty climate, cleanliness was very important to the Egyptians, and rich Egyptians had separate rooms for bathing. Rich or poor, everyone enjoyed a daily bath in the river or at home. Soap was a cream made of oil, lime, and perfume. After bathing, Egyptians rubbed their skin with sweet-smelling oil to keep their skin moist.

A wealthy man's villa

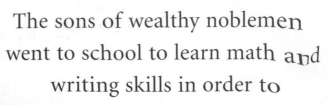

The sons of wealthy noblemen went to school to learn math and writing skills in order to become scribes. Boys started school when they were nine years old and continued for at least five years. They had to memorize more than 700 different hieroglyphic images just to write! Girls of this age were trained in music, dance, and duties of the home.

Hieroglyphics are carved into the clothing of an Egyptian youth in this ancient statue.

THE FIRST TOILET

A very simple toilet was often found in ancient Egyptian homes. The toilet was basically a seat placed over a large jar filled with sand.

CHAPTER III:

DYNASTIES AND THREE KINGDOMS

Around 3118 B.C.E., King Menes of Upper Egypt conquered Lower Egypt and formed the first national government with his capital in Memphis, near present-day Cairo. As Egypt's first pharaoh, his crown carried both the red and white symbols as a sign of the new unified Egypt. Menes began the first **dynasty**, and all rulers after him carried **Crook** and **Flail scepters** to show the pharaoh was both a shepherd and defender of his people. A pharaoh had total control of his country and could do as he wished because everyone and everything belonged to him.

With such a large area to rule, it was necessary for Egypt to be divided into **provinces** with appointed officials who acted like governors. During the next 400 years, the Egyptians developed a vast irrigation system, invented ox-drawn plows, and furthered their use of hieroglyphic record keeping.

A flail (left) and a crook (above right)

The **Old Kingdom** began with Dynasty III in 2686 B.C.E., and the next 500 years were known as The Pyramid Age. With a stable, centralized government, Egypt became richer. **Mastabas**, and later **pyramids**, were built as tombs for kings well in advance of their deaths. Trade extended as far as Lebanon, a country known for its prized cedar, and the country of Punt, present-day Somalia, for its fragrant **myrrh** trees. Large, organized armies defended Egypt's frontiers and trade routes. Egyptian craftsmen made fine works of art from local and imported resources. Scholars taught writing and studied astronomy, medicine, and math. The first record of surgery was written on an ancient Egyptian scroll.

The Great Pyramid is one of the wonders of the world. It was originally 490 feet (149 m) tall, and its base covers 31 acres (12.5 ha).

Around 2181 B.C.E., near the end of the Old Kingdom, several years of low floods led to drought and famine. Governors and priests fought among themselves as power shifted away from the pharaoh. Egypt's central government collapsed, and the country divided once again into separate provinces, each with its own ruler.

Eventually, princes from a region known as Thebes rose to power to reunite Egypt and created the **Middle Kingdom**, which lasted from 2133 B.C.E. through 1633 B.C.E. With peace restored between the provinces, Egypt's wealth and power grew. Trade not only increased along the Nile, but also spread to other countries along the eastern coast of the Mediterranean Sea and to the Middle East. Egyptians conquered gold-rich Nubia, present-day Sudan, and they built large fortresses to protect their territories. Arts, crafts, and literature were important, and the Egyptians valued justice and fairness for everyone. They respected those who were older for their wisdom and knowledge of tradition.

Pharaohs ruled their people with absolute power.

However, the pharaoh's power was only as good as the pharaoh himself. Weaker rulers could not keep the country united or defend its borders. A group of Asian settlers called **Hyksos** invaded and conquered the Nile Delta, splitting it from Upper Egypt. Lower Egyptians were now forced to pay **taxes** to their new rulers. In order to collect these taxes, government officials visited the farmers twice a year. During the first visit, they estimated how much harvest the farmer would produce and counted their animals. After the harvest, the official returned to take half of all that the farmer owned, even if the harvest was not as much as expected!

The Hyksos people brought horses and chariots to Egypt, which changed the way armies fought and people traveled. New and better weapons made of bronze replaced Egypt's older wooden and stone ones.

A two-horse war chariot

Theban princes were finally able to overthrow the Hyksos in 1567 B.C.E. and to begin what is now known as the Golden Age of Egypt, or the **New Kingdom**. The pharaohs of the New Kingdom were determined to create a vast empire. Armies reorganized and marched on lands as far south as modern-day Sudan and northeast into

Queen Hatshepsut

Mesopotamia. They conquered Palestine, Syria, and all lands west of the Euphrates River. Slaves, copper, gold, ivory, and ebony were collected as tributes and transported back to Egypt, making Egypt the strongest and wealthiest nation in the Middle East.

Some of Egypt's most famous pharaohs came from the New Kingdom. Queen Hatshepsut ruled from 1490 B.C.E. until 1468 B.C.E. and was one of only four women pharaohs out of a total of 270! During her 20-year rule, expeditions brought myrrh, gold, baboons, and ivory from Punt.

A carving made of alabaster and inlaid with precious stones and gold

King Akhenaten's name means "He who is of service to Aten." Aten is the Sun God.

Amenhotep IV, who ruled between 1363 and 1347 B.C.E., changed the course of Egypt's history by closing all temples and introducing the worship of one god, Aten. Amenhotep used his wealth to move Egypt's capital from **Thebes** to Akhertaten, which is now El Amarna, and changed his name to Akhenaten. These changes angered many Egyptians.

When King Tutankhamen came to the throne in 1332 B.C.E., he restored all the old gods and moved the capital back to Thebes. Rameses II reigned for 65 years between 1289 and 1224 B.C.E. and is known as a great warrior.

After Rameses II died, droughts and the resulting lack of grain brought unrest to Egypt. Struggles for power by priests and nobles broke the country into small states. Once divided, Egypt lost control of its territories, and its weakness attracted a series of invaders. During the next 700 years, Nubian, Assyrian, and Persian rulers conquered Egypt. Finally the famous Greek conqueror, Alexander the Great, added Egypt to his empire in 332 B.C.E.

The Temple of Rameses II at Abu Simbel

CHAPTER IV:

WHAT DID EGYPTIANS EAT?

Barley and **emmer**, a coarse wheat, were common at Egyptian meals, and both were used to make beer and bread. These grains were ground into flour between two heavy stones and mixed with water to make bread dough. Flavored with garlic or honey, the dough was baked in clay pots on a fire.

Egyptians enjoyed a varied diet. Lentils, beans, cucumbers, leeks, onions, peas, cabbage, and lettuce were a few of the vegetables they ate. Sweet and juicy fruits like dates, figs, pomegranates, melons, and grapes were at every meal. Grapes were grown, harvested, and made into wine for the wealthy. The grapes were placed in large tubs where "treaders" stomped the juice out of the grapes with their feet! The wines were then stored in clay jars with a label showing where the grapes were grown and when the wine was made.

Grapes (above) and wild ducks (left)

Common people used nets to catch fish and trap wild ducks, geese, and water birds along the marshes to supply the tables of the wealthy. In spite of the plentiful resources, the poor only ate fish, fowl, and meat on special occasions.

Domesticated cattle, oxen, sheep, goats, pigs, ducks, and geese supplied meat, milk, hides, and **dung** for cooking fuel. Birds were also raised on farms for their meat and eggs. Oxen pulling heavy loads and plows helped farmers increase their harvests.

Eggs (above) and domesticated pigs (below) were common to Egyptian farms.

FISHING BOATS ON THE NILE

Egyptians used small fishing boats made from papyrus reeds tied together. The boats floated because of the natural air pockets in the reeds.

Both as recreation and as a show of their skill, pharaohs and noblemen hunted, fished, and shot wild birds. After feasting on the meat, they decorated their homes with hides from rabbits, deer, **gazelles**, bulls, **oryx**, antelopes, hippopotamuses, elephants, and lions.

Fishermen in papyrus reed boats and fishing with nets

CHAPTER V

WHAT DID EGYPTIANS WEAR?

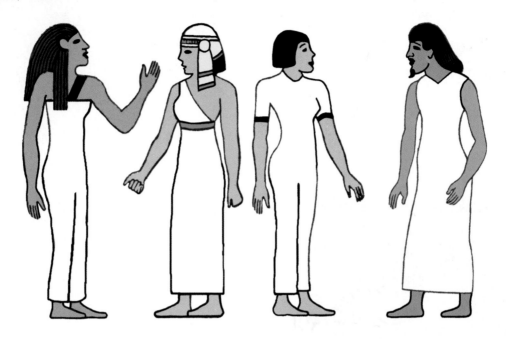

Common dress styles of ancient Egypt

Egyptians wore clothing made of finely woven linen for summer and a coarser version for extra warmth in winter. The men dressed in short skirts to their knees called **kilts**. The kilts of wealthy Egyptian men were pleated, and their sandals were made of leather. Most commoners went barefoot or wore simple sandals made from papyrus. Women wore long, straight dresses that were fitted and held up by straps. Noblewomen could afford more elaborate, beaded dresses. Kings and queens wore clothing decorated with colorful feathers, and many wore shawls.

Rich or poor, all Egyptians wore face paint because it was believed to have magical and healing powers. They spread eye paint made from green **malachite** on their eyelids. They ground a gray lead ore into fine powder and mixed it with oil to make an eye color

Statue of female with eye paint

called **kohl**. They outlined their upper and lower eyelids all the way out to the sides of their faces. Some thought the eye paint would make their eyesight better or prevent eye infections. The black eye paint actually helped to protect them from the intense desert sunlight.

Statue of an Egyptian nobleman

Egyptians mixed water with a fine red, clay powder to color their lips and cheeks. A reddish brown dye from **henna** plants was used to color their fingernails. Makeup was stored in special boxes that they even carried to parties and would place under their chairs.

Hairstyles in ancient Egypt were kept short, perhaps because of the intense heat and for reasons of cleanliness. Children wore pigtails, and boys' heads were shaved except for one braid they wore on the side. It was common for both men and women to shave their heads and wear wigs made of sheep's wool or human hair.

An Egyptian couple (above) in common dress. Examples of hairstyles (below).

CHAPTER VI:
TRADE AND COMMERCE

A caravan of camels in the desert

In Ancient Egypt trade goods came in and out of the country as gifts between the pharaohs and rulers of other foreign countries. Egypt had plenty of resources that other countries wanted such as grain and other foodstuffs, copper, malachite, gemstones, and **natron**. In return, Egypt brought in timber, iron, silver, tin, and lead. Long, straight timbers came from Byblos in Phoenicia for building ships, houses, temples, and palaces. Fragrant sap from the famous cedars of Lebanon helped to preserve Egyptian **mummies**.

Travel was often by foot or camel caravans over desert land, but the Nile River was the highway that joined the country from the Mediterranean Sea to the rest of Africa. Gold, jewels, ivory, and even wild animals were transported to the great palaces of Egyptian noblemen. Leopards and monkeys were often kept as pets of the wealthy. On any day, boats of all shapes and sizes crowded the busy waterways of the Nile River.

Early boats were made of papyrus reeds, but by 3200 B.C.E. a fleet of ships built of wooden planks and powered by sails made journeys to the Phoenician coast, Cyprus, and the Aegean Sea. These vessels were filled with copper, oils, sweet-smelling wood, lumber, resin, wine, opium, and finely crafted items as gifts and tributes from occupied lands. Wealthy noble families took their own ornate boats up and down the Nile River while entertaining.

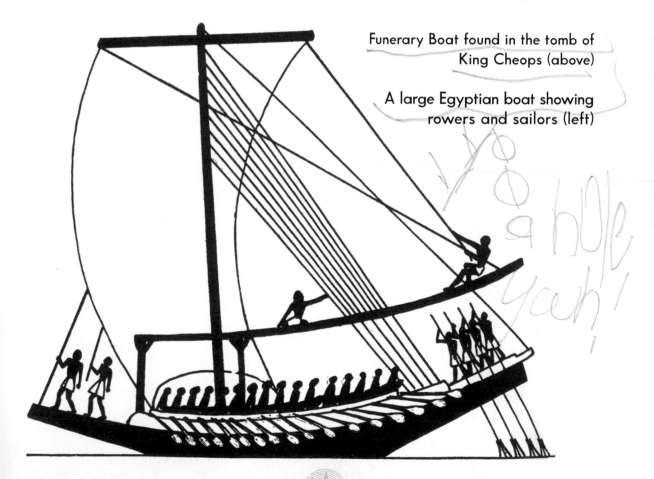

Funerary Boat found in the tomb of King Cheops (above)

A large Egyptian boat showing rowers and sailors (left)

CHAPTER VII:
ART AND ARCHITECTURE

Giant pyramids rose up from the desert sands and remain today as one of the greatest mysteries of Egypt. While they were still living, pharaohs built these enormous tombs for themselves, their families, servants, and all the belongings they would need in the afterlife, called the **Next World**.

During the Old Kingdom, the tombs or mastabas were large, rectangular stone buildings. Stone columns with their tops carved to look like palms or papyrus decorated the outside of these massive structures. Workers dug deep tunnels beneath the mastaba to a secret chamber where the important nobles and kings were buried.

Later in the Old Kingdom and throughout the Middle Kingdom, pyramids replaced mastabas. The first pyramids were step-sided. Later the pyramids had smooth sides and were covered with white limestone, so they glistened in the desert landscape.

The pyramids of Kings Khufu, Khafre, and Mankaure at Giza

30

Pyramids were made of blocks of stone and took thousands of men many years to complete. A large square base created a stable structure with most of the building materials in the lower half of the structure. As the pyramid grew, each stone was cut, brought to the site by boat, and then pulled or pushed up a long ramp to build the top of the pyramid.

The most famous pyramids are located west of the Nile River in Giza. There, three kings and their queens were buried, where they were guarded by the **Great Sphinx**. Historians estimate it took more than 20,000 workers almost 20 years to complete the largest of these pyramids for King Khufu. Commoners, and later criminals and slaves, made up the workforce on these projects.

A ramp on the side of a pyramid

MYSTERIOUS ENGINEERING FEAT

Blocks of stone weighing more than 2.5 tons (2,300 kg) had to be moved up the pyramid as it grew in height. It is thought that ramps were built along the sides and then sprayed with water to make it easier for the men to drag the stones. It took as many as 10 men to drag one stone up the ramp. Ramps were built on each side of the pyramid at different levels as needed.

Raised roadways connected the giant pyramids to the temple and other structures of an entire burial complex. Smaller pyramids were built for members of the family and nobles. Mastabas made of brick or stone were still used as grave markers and storage rooms for offerings for the dead and housed the souls of the nobles.

The mask of King Tutankhamen

TUTANKHAMEN'S TOMB

King Tutankhamen was only 18 years old when he died. His tomb survived grave robbers and was discovered mostly intact in 1922. The boy king was protected by a nest of human-shaped mummy cases, one placed inside the other. His face was covered with a mask made of gold. The final case was placed in a large stone box called a **sarcophagus**. Found in the tomb were 116 baskets of fruit, 40 jars of wine, boxes of meat, chariots, fine robes, musical instruments, and furniture.

The Great Sphinx

Buried riches in the tombs tempted thieves, and as a result many pyramids were robbed of their treasures. The pharaohs of the New Kingdom decided to cut their tombs deep inside cliffs on the west bank of Thebes in an area known as the **Valley of the Kings**. To discourage tomb robbers, great treasures were buried with the kings in secret chambers that could only be reached through a maze of tunnels.

PYRAMIDS OF GIZA AND THE GREAT SPHINX

The largest pyramid of Giza was finished in 2538 B.C.E. for King Khufu and was built with more than two million blocks of stone. It rose 480 feet (146 m) high and was covered with white limestone plaster. Guarding the site of the three pyramids was the Great Sphinx, which measured 70 feet (21 m) high and 237 feet (73 m) long. The Great Sphinx has the head of a king.

CATS

Cats were considered to be sacred and to have magical powers. They protected the home and children from danger and helped crops to grow. Some were even mummified and buried with their owners. Cats were so important that they even had their own god, Bastet. Killing a cat could be punished by death!

Special craftsmen called mummy-makers preserved the bodies of royalty and rich people to keep them from decaying. Preparation and preservation of the body could take up to 70 days. The brain was removed first by pulling it through the nose with a long bronze hook. Then the lungs, liver, stomach, and intestines were removed. These organs were put in a **canopic jar** filled with natron and later placed in the tomb with the body.

During mummification, the body was covered in natron for 40 days. After the body had completely dried out, it was rubbed with cedar oil and resin to soften it. For the next 15 days, the mummy-maker stuffed the body with linen and spices and wrapped it in linen bandages.

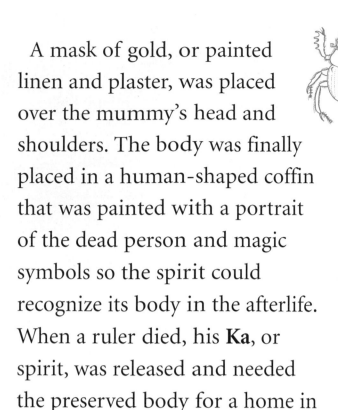

A mask of gold, or painted linen and plaster, was placed over the mummy's head and shoulders. The body was finally placed in a human-shaped coffin that was painted with a portrait of the dead person and magic symbols so the spirit could recognize its body in the afterlife. When a ruler died, his **Ka**, or spirit, was released and needed the preserved body for a home in the Next World.

The sarcophagus of Tutankhamen

AMULETS

Charms and **amulets** were wrapped between the folds of linen around the body. These charms were for protection, and most were shaped like a beetle, called a **scarab**. Scarabs represented the god, Khepri, who pushed the Sun around the Earth.

SLAVES FOR THE SOUL

Shabti were slaves for the soul and would come to life on the command of Osiris to perform tasks for the dead person in the afterlife. The Opening of the Mouth Ceremony was believed to give the dead the power to eat, breathe, and move in the afterlife.

Anubis was the god of mummification and guarded of the resting places of the departed.

A funeral was held for the dead. Mourners, priests, and possessions crossed the Nile with the coffin, which was then pulled by oxen over stony ground in a boat-shaped sled to the tomb. Women could be heard weeping and wailing. The final ceremony was performed at the tomb door before the mummy was put to rest in a nest of coffins inlaid with gold and semiprecious stones. A statuette that looked like the deceased was placed in the tomb along with shabti figures.

Once the souls finished their journey to the Next World, in order for them to enter they had to answer questions about their actions on earth. More than 200 spells written in the **Book of the Dead** were there to help them. Finally, standing in front of Osiris, a person's heart was weighed against a feather that represented truth. If the scale balanced, the soul would have good life and eternal joy. If the heart weighed more than the feather, then the "Swallowing Monster," a combination of crocodile, lion, and hippopotamus that sat by the scale, would gobble it up.

Because only pharaohs were believed to have an afterlife, the souls of nobles did not journey to the Next World. Their souls continued to live in the mastabas and required daily offerings of food and drink. Common people were buried in holes in the sand where the families did the best they could to make the person comfortable.

Papyrus painted with hieroglyphics shows Egyptian gods blessing the king.

CHAPTER IX

THE PEOPLE TODAY

Today many people have left the farms in hopes of finding work in cities.

Today Egypt occupies the northeastern area of Africa with a small portion called the Sinai Peninsula actually being in Asia. For years Egypt was a kingdom until it became a **republic** in 1952 with its official name, the Arab Republic of Egypt. Almost all of Egypt's 72,534,000 people live along the Nile River or along the Suez Canal, the country's other important waterway.

Egypt's population has continued to grow, and more people have moved from the rural areas to the cities looking for work. Lifestyles in the cities are very different from those on the farms. In the cities attractive houses can be seen next to poorer areas, and lack of housing in the crowded cities is a serious problem.

It was necessary for the government to build a system of roads, railroads, and ferries as populations grew. Now cars and freight trucks travel on the roads and inner city highways. There are buses, taxis, trains, an underground train in Cairo, tramways, cars, and Nile River ferries. The Nile is still a common method of travel in Egypt where people get from place to place in small, open sailboats.

A bridge in a modern Egyptian city

Most of the people consider themselves Arabs and speak Arabic, with English as their second language. French is sometimes heard in the cities. More than 90% of Egyptians are followers of Islam, a religion that influences their way of life and traditions.

ASWAN HIGH DAM

Built in 1971, the Aswan High Dam on the Nile River in southern Egypt is one of the world's largest dams. The dam is 11,811 feet (3,600 m) long, 3,215 feet (980 m) wide at the base, 131 feet (40 m) wide at the crest, and 364 feet (111 m) tall.

Clothing worn by Egyptians shows their different ways of life. In the cities, the people are dressed in much the same way as in the United States and Europe. Rural villagers and poorer city dwellers wear more traditional clothing. Men wear long pants and a long, full shirtlike garment. Women wear long, flowing gowns in dark or bright colors. Many men grow their beards and wear small hats as symbols of their religious beliefs. Islamic women wear robes and cover their heads and arms with a veil.

The Nile River continues to support agriculture, which is the main source of income for farmers and for Egypt. Cotton is the most important crop, but corn, fruits, rice, sugarcane, and wheat are used in the country, as well as exported. Since the 1900s, more machines have been used on farms. Yet much of the work is still done by hand, and it is common to see donkeys, water buffaloes, and camels used for heavy tasks.

The entrance obelisk at the Temple of Luxor shows deeply carved hieroglyphs.

Manufacturing has expanded, and cement, cotton fabrics, and processed foods are the main industries. Petroleum and the Aswan High Dam on the Nile River are sources of energy and power for the country.

Sunset on the rooftops in a modern Egyptian city

Many of Egypt's ancient monuments are a main attraction for travelers from all areas. Tourists are drawn to the beautiful weather, sandy beaches, and water activities such as surfing, snorkeling, diving, and water games year-round.

Ancient Egypt developed a great culture more than 5,000 years ago. Early Egyptian forms of writing and mathematics and the creation of a national government paved the way to the Egypt we see today. Just like all cultures, we understand more about the people today by studying their history from ancient times.

A TIMELINE OF THE
HISTORY OF EGYPT

5000 B.C.E. The Sahara Desert, which was once green, is still fertile in parts and there is evidence of cattle herders in the area. As the Sahara dries, many people migrate to the Nile Valley.

3300 B.C.E. Hieroglyphic writing develops.

3118 B.C.E. Menes, first king of Dynasty 1, unites Upper and Lower Egypt.

2686-2181 B.C.E. Old Kingdom in Egypt. Dynasties III to VI. Known for the construction of great pyramids, including the Giza pyramid during Dynasty IV.

2133-1633 B.C.E. Middle Kingdom in Egypt. Period of great prosperity during Dynasties XI-XIII.

1674-1567 B.C.E. Hyksos rulers form a dynasty that rules Egypt for 100 years.

1567-1085 B.C.E.   Hyksos driven out and Egypt reunited as New Kingdom in Egypt; Dynasties XVIII-XX.

1085-656 B.C.E.   Dynasties XXI-XXV. Egypt begins its decline and is conquered by foreign countries.

525-404 B.C.E.   First occupation of Egypt by Persia and Cyrus the Great.

343-332 B.C.E.   Egypt conquered and occupied by Persia.

332 B.C.E.   Egypt conquered by Alexander the Great.

30 B.C.E.   Egypt becomes a Roman Province.

GLOSSARY

Amulets: Magic charms made of gold, stone, clay, or wax that were believed to protect the wearer from evil. In ancient Egypt they were placed between layers of mummy's bandages.

Book of the Dead: A collection of prayers, magic spells, and songs that guided and protected the soul in its journey to the afterlife.

Canopic Jars: Jars used to store the internal organs removed during embalming. Each jar had a stopper in the shape of a head, either human, jackal, baboon, or falcon.

Crook and Flail Scepters: Symbols of Egyptian pharaohs. The crook was a long staff with one end shaped like a hook used by shepherds. The flail is a tool with a handle and free-swinging stick used for beating.

Dung: Animal manure.

Dynasty: A succession of powerful rulers all from one family.

Emmer: A type of wheat with red kernels mostly grown for feed for livestock.

Famine: A severe shortage of food that results in starvation and death for the people.

Ferment: The process by which sugar breaks down into alcohol.

Gazelle: A small, swift, and graceful antelope found in Africa and Asia.

Great Sphinx: The statue that guards the three pyramids at Giza. It has a lion's body and the head of a man.

Henna: A shrub that grows in North Africa and Asia with fragrant white and red flowers used to make a reddish brown dye.

Hieroglyphics: Writing system using picture symbols in Ancient Egypt.

Hyksos: A mixed group of Asian people who appeared along the Nile Delta during the Old Kingdom.

Inundation: The rising of a body of water and its flooding onto normally dry land.

Ka: The soul of a dead person in Ancient Egypt believed to be able to live in a statue of that person after death.

Kilts: Short skirts worn by Egyptian men.

Kohl: A makeup used by Egyptians to darken the rims of their eyelids.

Lotus: White water lily of Egypt and southeastern Africa important in religion and art. The lily was a symbol of regeneration.

Malachite: A mineral containing bright green copper.

Mastaba: An ancient Egyptian mud-brick tomb with a rectangular base and sloping sides and flat roof.

Middle Kingdom: A period of ancient Egyptian history from the 11th to the 14th dynasty.

Mummy: A body treated for burial with preservatives in the manner of ancient Egypt.

Myrrh: A tree of eastern Africa and Asia that has a gum used in perfume and incense.

Natron: A white, yellow, or gray mineral consisting of sodium carbonate and once used in embalming.

New Kingdom: A period in the history of ancient Egypt, from the 18th to the 20th dynasty.

Next World: In ancient Egypt, the place

where souls of pharaohs lived after death.

Old Kingdom: The period of ancient Egyptian history from the 4th to 8th dynasties, when the capital was at Memphis and the great pyramids were built.

Oryx: A large African antelope with long, straight, nearly upright horns.

Papyrus: The plant used to make paper; also the kind of paper made from the papyrus plant.

Pharaoh: Most powerful person in ancient Egypt and who was the political and religious leader.

Provinces: Regions controlled by an appointed governor.

Pyramid: A huge stone tomb of ancient Egyptian royalty with a square base and triangular walls that slope to meet in a point at the top.

Republic: A form of government whose head is not a king or queen.

Sarcophagus: An ancient stone or marble coffin, often decorated with sculpture and inscriptions.

Scarab: A large dung beetle considered sacred in ancient Egypt. The insects rolled balls of dung to provide a home for their larvae.

Shabti: Images of slaves for the souls.

Taxes: An involuntary fee in the form of crops, goods, or gifts paid by an individual to a government.

Thebes: Capital city of ancient Egypt located on both sides of the Nile River south of present-day Cairo. It is across the Nile from the Valley of the Kings.

Valley of the Kings: The burial site on the west bank of the Nile for many pharaohs of the New Kingdom.

Books of Interest

Chisholm, Jane. *The Usborne Book of World History Dates.* New York: Scholastic Incorporated, 1998.

Crisp, Peter. *e.guides Mummy.* New York: DK Publishing, Inc., 2004.

Martell, Hazel. *The Kingfisher Book of the Ancient World.* New York: Larousse Kingfisher Chambers, Incorporated, 1995.

Harrison, James. *Discovering Ancient Egypt.* New York: Sterling Publishing Company, 2004.

Jackson, Kevin and Stamp, Jonathan. *Building the Great Pyramid.* New York: Firefly Books, Ltd, 2003.

Malam, John. *Mummies.* Boston: Kingfisher Publications, 2003.

Millard, Anne and Vanags, Patricia. *The Usborne Book of World History.* London: Usborne Publishing Ltd., 1985.

Silverman, David P. *Ancient Egypt.* New York: Oxford University Press, 1997.

Steele, Philip. *The Best Book of Mummies.* New York: Kingfisher Publications, 1998.

Websites of Interest

http://www.ancientegypt.co.uk

http://www.civilization.ca/civil/egypt/egypte.html#menu

http://www.mummy.dke-guides.com

INDEX

Katherine E. Reece is a native of Georgia, where she grew up in a small town located in the foothills of the Blue Ridge Mountains. She has traveled throughout the United States, Europe, Australia, and New Zealand. Katherine completed her Bachelor of Fine Arts with an emphasis in studio art at the University of Colorado in Boulder, Colorado, where she now resides. Her extensive studies in art history gives her an appreciation for all that can be learned about the culture, beliefs, and traditions of ancient civilizations from the architecture, artifacts, and recordings that have been preserved through the centuries.